ENDURING LOVE

A SPOUSE'S VOYAGE THROUGH GRIEF

AYUSHI JAIN

Made with ♥ on the Notion Press Platform
www.notionpress.com

Praise for the book

Captivating and heartwarming, **"Enduring Love: A Spouse's Voyage Through Grief"** is a powerful tribute to the enduring love and unwavering commitment of my parents. Through the pages of this beautifully crafted story, we are taken on a poignant journey, witnessing the remarkable strength of a couple who stood resolutely by each other's side in the face of adversity. My mother's selfless sacrifices for her children serve as a shining example of maternal devotion and resilience. This touching narrative reminds us of the enduring power of love and family bonds, leaving readers inspired and deeply moved. **"Enduring Love: A Spouse's Voyage Through Grief"** is a heartfelt celebration of the extraordinary within the ordinary, a tale that will stay with you long after the final page."

AYUSHI JAIN,

Daughter of Mr. Sharad & Rekha Jain

Contents

Contents

Acknowledgements

I would like to express my heartfelt gratitude to all those who contributed to the creation of "Enduring Love: A Spouse's Voyage Through Grief." This book is not just a story; it's a testament to the unwavering love and strength that my parents exhibited throughout their lives.

First and foremost, I want to thank my parents for sharing their remarkable journey with us and for being a constant source of inspiration. Your love and commitment to each other, even in the face of adversity, have touched our hearts and taught us valuable lessons about the enduring power of love and family bonds.

I extend my gratitude to all those who supported and encouraged us throughout the process of bringing this book to life. To our friends, family, and well-wishers, your belief in the importance of this story has been a driving force.

I also want to acknowledge the readers who have picked up "Enduring Love" and allowed my parents' story to touch your hearts. Your support is what allows this tale to endure, and I hope it continues to inspire and resonate with you.

Lastly, a special thanks to those who were there for us during the difficult times, especially my mother, whose sacrifices and

devotion are at the heart of this narrative. Your strength and love are the pillars upon which this book is built.

"Enduring Love" is a celebration of the extraordinary found within the ordinary, and it is a tribute to love that transcends grief and challenges. May it serve as a reminder of the enduring power of love, resilience, and family bonds. Thank you all for being a part of this journey.

With profound gratitude,

Ayushi Jain

Special Note

Thanks……

In the echoes of time, where memories reside,
A tale of love, with parents as my guide.
Through storms and stars, they held my hand,
Crafting dreams, on life's shifting sand.
My mother, a guardian spirit in the sky,
Though absent, her love will never die.
Her whispers linger in each gentle breeze,
Guiding me through life's uncertainties.
Beside me, my father, a pillar strong and tall,
In his shadow, I learned to stand, to walk, to fall.
Their unwavering support, a beacon bright,
Ignites my path with eternal light.
In their love, I find my endless sea,
For what I am, I owe to them, eternally.
With heartfelt thanks, my soul takes flight,
To parents, my stars, my eternal light.

1. Love Story Born in '92: Parents' Enduring Love

In '92, a love story began to bloom,
My Dad's heart found his destined room.
A first sight love, a tale so sweet,
In Mother's eyes, his heart did beat.

In '92, their love took flight,
Two souls united, shining so bright.
A love story, pure and divine,
In my Mother's eyes, my Dad's sunshine.

Through the years, their love did grow,
In my Mother's arms, he found his glow.
A connection so deep, a love so true,
In those moments, their journey they knew.

From that first glance, a bond was formed,
In my Mother's love, his heart was warmed.
Together they walked, hand in hand,

Building a life on love's gentle strand.

So I cherish the love that brought me here,
For in their love, there's nothing to fear.
A first sight love, a love so grand,
In my parents' hearts, forever will stand.

2. Promises and Perseverance: Love amidst Family Struggles

In the glow of vows unwavering and sure,
A challenge arose, a test to endure.
Parents vowed to stand close and fast,
But in-laws' objections, a shadow they cast.

A union tested by familial strife,
A husband supporting his cherished wife.
In the midst of conflicts, they held their ground,
With love and determination, their bond was found.

Though the path was rocky, and tensions ran high,
In each other's love, they reached for the sky.
Promises made, they knew not in vain,
Through trials and tribulations, they'd remain.

In-laws' opinions came and went,
But the love they shared, it steadfastly leant.
With united hearts, they weathered the storm,

In each other's embrace, they found their warm.

So, in the face of challenges, they'd endure,
With promises kept, and love so pure.
For in the end, what truly did matter,
Was the love they shared, growing stronger, not shatter..

3. Love across Distances: A Timeless Bond

In distant lands, their paths did part,
A sacrifice made, but not from the heart.
He went to Mumbai, a bustling array,
While she was in MP, teaching each day.

With only one saree, simple and fair,
She wore it with grace, with love to spare.
Their meetings were rare, months apart,
In an era of PCOs, where voices were art.

No mobile phones then, no texts or call,
Yet their love persisted, unbreakable thrall.
In reminiscence, they found strength each day,
Through distance and time, their love held its sway.

In six or eight months, their hearts took flight,
In those precious moments, their love burned bright.
Distance couldn't wither what their hearts could sever,
Their love, a bond that nothing could ever.

Through trials and tribulations, they stood so tall,
Their love story enduring, surpassing them all.
In a world so different, where love was the tether,
My parents, a testament, forever and together.

4. Bound by Love: Together Through Thick and Thin

Through the years, their love did grow,
A bond so deep, a radiant glow.
They decided one day, come what may,
To share life's journey, side by side, they'd stay.

They said, "We'll eat together, just us two,
Share every meal, love tried and true.
In good and bad, in joy and strife,
We'll navigate this precious life."

With this vow, they took their stand,
Hand in hand, in love's gentle hand.
Through thick and thin, their hearts entwined,
In unity and love, their souls aligned.

No matter the trials, they'd endure,
Their love, steadfast, strong, and pure.
With every bite of sweetcorn, a shared delight,

In each other's presence, love was there, day and night.

Years passed, their love did deepen,
Promises kept, forever, they'd keep on keepin'.
In a world of togetherness, they'd always be,
A testament to love's enduring decree.

5. Love and Resilience in a World of Hunger

In a town where hunger gnawed each day,
My parents found their way.
With bellies empty, dreams in their eyes,
They faced the world with heartfelt sighs.

In hardship's grip, they shared a single grain,
Two hearts, one sweetcorn, eased the hunger's pain.
Her hands, with love and care, did sew,
Petticoats, a lifeline, through the tough times flow.

Potato chips, a humble start, she'd sell,
With hope and strength, their lives began to swell.
In unity and toil, they rose above,
A story of resilience, bound by their love.

Hand in hand, they ventured forth,
Through hardships and trials, proving their worth.
With love and hope, their hearts grew strong,
In a world where food was scarce, they'd belong.

He, brave and steadfast as a tree,
She, a beacon of strength, you see.
Together, they weathered the stormy skies,
Their unity and love, a precious prize.

They shared what little they had to eat,
In times of scarcity, made ends meet.
With laughter and stories, they found delight,
In each other's presence, day and night.

Though hunger's shadow hung overhead,
They cherished the moments, where love spread.
For in this town with limited fare,
Their bond and love were beyond compare.

Through thick and thin, they stood as one,
He and his beloved wife, under the sun.
In a world where food was a fleeting treat,
Their love and resilience couldn't be beat.

6. Unbreakable Bond: Parents Who Weathered Life Together

In the storms of life, they stood as one,
Two hearts, together, when the day was done.
Through thick and thin, in trials and strife,
They carved a path, creating their life.

No one else by their side, just hand in hand,
Facing the world, they made their stand.
When darkness fell, and the night grew long,
In each other's arms, they found they were strong.

With no one to lean on, but each other's grace,
They painted their love in life's empty space.
In solitude and silence, they found their way,
Building a bond that would forever stay.

Through laughter and tears, they shared their dreams,
In the face of adversity, they were a team.
For the love they held was their guiding star,

In a world that seemed distant, they were never far.

So here's to the parents, unwavering and true,
Who weathered life's storms with strength they knew.
In their unity and love, we find the grace,
Of two souls together, in life's embrace.

7. A Growing Love: Welcoming a New Baby

In the second year of love's embrace,
A precious gift, a new smiling face.
One year had passed since their love took flight,
Now a baby arrived, a source of pure delight.

In the cradle of love, this child would grow,
Nurtured and cherished, in their hearts aglow.
With tiny fingers and innocent eyes,
A new chapter began, beneath the skies.

In the warmth of their love, this baby would thrive,
With every coo and every cry, they'd strive.
To provide comfort, and love so rare,
In the circle of family, a bond they'd share.

One year of parenthood, a journey begun,
With the rising of the morning sun.
In the second year, their love did expand,
A family of three, hand in hand.

So they embraced this new role with grace,
In their hearts, a smile on each face.
For in this little one, a future they'd see,
Bound by love, a cherished family.

8. Two Little Blessings: Brothers' Bond of Mischief and Love

After two years of joy, a new delight,
Another baby boy, so full of light.
From the moment he arrived, a bundle of joy,
A little one, full of laughter, their new baby boy.

With mischief in his eyes and a mischievous grin,
He charmed their hearts, a playful spin.
From day one, his spirit shone so bright,
A naughty little boy, pure delight.

His giggles filled the air, his laughter rang,
In the midst of chaos, his innocence sang.
Though he tested their patience day by day,
In their hearts, his love held sway.

Two years apart, these brothers so dear,
Creating memories they'd forever hold near.
In the tapestry of family, their bonds were sewn,

Two little boys, their love had grown.

As time marched on, their laughter would bloom,
In the story of their lives, there was always room.
For the mischievous one, and the one before,
In their hearts, more love to explore.

9. Completing the Family: A Daughter's Arrival

Three years had passed, a journey in time,
With two little boys, their hearts did chime.
But in the year 1998 , a new chapter unfurled,
As they welcomed a daughter into their world.

With eyes like stars, and a heart so pure,
A precious girl, their love would secure.
In their arms, she found her place,
A cherished blessing, a smiling grace.

Her laughter, a melody, in the family's song,
A daughter, a sister, where she belonged.
In three years' time, their family grew,
With love overflowing, a bond so true.

Brothers and sister, hand in hand,
They explored the world, a united band.
In the years ahead, their story to write,
With love and laughter, their hearts unite.

Three years of waiting, their patience tried,
But in the end, their hearts were tied.
To their little girl, so sweet and new,
A love so strong, forever true.

10. Sibling Bond: Sparkle Fevicol and Playful Teasing

In our family of five, a perfect blend,
Mom, Dad, brothers, and a sister, a friend.
Yet in the midst of our love's gentle swirl,
A playful teasing, a brotherly pearl.

When stubbornness gripped me, oh so tight,
My brother's remedy, a mischievous delight.
With sparkle Fevicol, he'd gently tease,
Dropping it on my hair, with laughter and ease.

A sparkling confession, a bond so sweet,
In those moments, our hearts would meet.
Through playful pranks, love's thread did twine,
A sibling connection, forever to shine.

In our perfect family, love's always there,
A mix of fun, laughter, and care.
With sticky memories, our hearts entwined,

In a world of siblings, love's design.

So in the tale of our family's lore,
Sparkle Fevicol brought laughter galore.
A brother's tease, a sister's grin,
In this playful love, we'd always win.

11. Mischievous Directions: A Childhood Tale

In childhood's realm of playful schemes,
Where mischief danced in youthful dreams,
A prank was played, a tale to tell,
Of directions gone awry, a moment to quell.

A customer in need, for stones that ache,
To find the homeopathic cure, his journey did take.
My brother, a merely four, with eyes so bright,
Stood by my uncle's shop, a mischievous sight.

"Take him in your lap," my uncle did decree,
"He'll guide you well, just wait and see."
With trust in his eyes, the customer complied,
Not knowing what mischief my brother would ride.

He followed the directions, so earnest and clear,
But my brother's plan was far from sincere.
At the final turn, a mischievous hand,

Pointed straight ward, in a misdirecting stand.

Round and round, the customer did roam,
Lost in streets, far from our home.
From morning till evening, a futile quest,
He returned in despair, feeling quite stressed.

My uncle's gentle slap, a lesson so wise,
Tears in my brother's mischievous eyes.
"Follow him now," my uncle implored,
And the lost soul's journey found its reward.

In the end, the destination was found,
Through playful antics, and laughter's sound.
A childhood tale, in memory enshrined,
Of youthful pranks, and mischief's bind.

In the tapestry of our family lore,
This tale lives on, forevermore.
Of directions askew, a mischievous twist,
A lesson learned, in moments like this.

12. A Brother's Change of Heart: From Veggie Hater to Craving Greens

In the family, the oldest baby was the quiet one,
Focused on his dreams, a rising sun.
A career-driven soul, so determined and bright,
But green veggies to him were a constant fight.

He'd push them away, those greens so mean,
With a stubbornness, his plate kept clean.
But as he left for studies, far from home's embrace,
A longing grew for Mom's vegetable grace.

When he returned, with a smile so wide,
He asked for bottle gourd, a humble stride.
I chuckled and teased, "Is this really you?"
He laughed, "Yes, it's true, I've changed my view."

For distance had softened his stubborn heart,
And family's love played its magical part.
He missed those flavors from home's sweet pot,

A lesson in longing, his taste buds caught.

In the laughter and love of that moment so dear,
We cherished the change, so crystal clear.
A brother transformed, his tastes renewed,
In the bonds of family, love pursued.

So, here's to the brother, both old and new,
Who found love for veggies, a change he'd pursue.
In the circle of home, where memories reside,
Laughter and love, on this journey, we ride.

13. A Brother's Summer Gifts: Tokens of Love

In the days of youth, so bright and warm,
When summer's embrace would transform,
Our home with laughter, joy, and cheer,
As my brother's love drew near.

From a distant place, he'd journey back,
With treasures held in a humble sack,
His savings, scraped from meager sum,
To bring us gifts, make our hearts overcome.

Eight hundred rupees, a world to him,
Covering costs, room, and board so grim,
But from those scraps, he'd set apart,
A gesture of love, a gift from the heart.

With a heart of gold and love so pure,
He'd choose for each a gift, ensure,
His mother and sister, smiles would find,
In the treasures from his heart, so kind.

The mess fee saved, the room cost too,
Travel expenses, so much he'd eschew,
To bring us joy, and warmth anew,
In the simplest gifts, his love would ensue.

For my brother, in his sacrifice,
He painted love in a priceless guise,
A lesson learned, a memory made,
In the treasures brought in a summer's shade.

His savings, a testament to his care,
A bond so deep, love beyond compare,
In his sacrifices, we'd clearly see,
The depth of love, a family's key.

In memories now, those gifts still shine,
A love that endures through the sands of time,
From my brother's heart, so pure and true,
A summer's gift, a love we always knew.

14. Memories of Almond Halwa

In days of old, when youth was pure,
We slept upon the floor, secure,
A family bound, a love so tight,
As morning's first soft rays took flight.

In that dim room, we lay in rest,
Four souls within, all truly blessed,
The floor our bed, the dreams our guide,
As childhood's innocence did ride.

The dawn would break with golden hue,
And school called out, our journey grew,
We'd rise with eagerness and cheer,
For learning's path was always near.

But oh, the magic in those morns,
When almond halwa in small forms,
A teaspoon's worth, a treasure sweet,
Our mother's love, in each small treat.

With humble means, she spread her grace,
A spoonful shared in that small space,
Our hearts were warmed, our spirits light,
In that fleeting moment, pure delight.

The taste of love, so rich and warm,
Within that halwa, a childhood charm,
A memory cherished, sweet and true,
In the simple joys, we always knew.

15. A Bond: The Best and Happiest Family

The firstborn, a pathfinder, ventured away,
For studies and dreams, a new light of day.
Though distance was far, and home not in sight,
He'd visit sometimes, in the soft evening light.

Financial strains, tickets were dear,
Yet when he'd return, it was cause for cheer.
Three siblings together, hearts intertwined,
In the tapestry of family, love defined.

Years swiftly passed, a life on the wing,
Three siblings studying, a song they'd sing.
In laughter and learning, they'd find their way,
A close-knit family, come what may.

Financial hurdles, but love was the key,
In the warmth of their bond, they'd all agree.
The best of times, a happy family, they'd say,
In each other's presence, day by day.

Through trials and triumphs, they'd stand as one,
In the journey of life, a race they'd run.
For in sibling love, they'd find their glee,
The best and happiest family, you see.

16. Sacrifice of Silence: A Mother's Unspoken Love

In silence, she carried a heavy load,
A secret, a fear, in her heart it flowed.
A tiny tumor, a pea's small size,
But a weighty truth behind her eyes.

She chose not to burden, not to share,
With her beloved, in tender care.
To the doctor, she went alone,
Brave and quiet, her strength was shown.

A second tumor, an added weight,
But still, she chose a hidden gate.
For she knew the cost, the lacs it'd demand,
Her love for her family, she'd carefully planned.

In her silence, her love did speak,
A sacrifice made, from fear she'd seek.
To protect her family, she'd bear the pain,
In her heart, love's gentle reign.

A mother's love, both fierce and true,
In the choices made, her love she'd imbue.
In silence, she carried the weight,
For her family's sake, a loving trait.

So, in her quiet strength, she'd remain,
A hero in shadows, in love's domain.
A tale of sacrifice, unspoken and deep,
In her heart, her love's promise, she'd keep.

17. A Quest for Healing: Homeopathic Hope and Challenges

In the realm of alternative care, she sought,
A homeopathic doctor, remedies they brought.
Leaves, a secret cure, for the tumor's plight,
With hope in her heart, she followed the light.

A paste of leaves, applied with care,
To heal the tumor, a burden to bear.
But as days passed by, it took a turn,
The tumor's growth, a cause for concern.

A remedy tried, with faith so strong,
But sometimes, the path can be wrong.
In the quest for healing, a brave endeavor,
Yet sometimes, it takes a different measure.

In her journey for health, she'd strive,
With love and courage, she'd stay alive.

For in the face of trials, she'd find her way,
In the hope of a brighter, healthier day.

18. A Mother's Sacrifice: Love's Crossroads and Heartbreak

In a moment of truth, Mum secret was revealed,
The tumor's presence, its fate now sealed.
Dad's concern, a plea to the best of care,
But her love for her family, a cross to bear.

With expenses looming, her son's dreams at stake,
She chose to refuse, her decision to make.
"I would die if I go," those words she spoke,
A heavy truth, in her love, it woke.

Dad's heart, shattered in that moment so stark,
A life's crossroads, emotions leaving a mark.
In the face of love and sacrifice, they stood,
A family united, the way that love should.

Through trials and tribulations, they'd find their way,
In the light of love's promise, come what may.

A mum's sacrifice, a dad's pain,
In their unity, strength they'd gain.

19. A Mother's Journey: Love, Loss, and Healing

With arguments and worries, she'd finally agree,
To face the unknown, for her family.
In the heart of Delhi, a battle did unfold,
Mum's health, a story to be told.

To the best hospital, dad would take,
For chemotherapy's journey, a road to make.
He didn't reveal the truth, he'd just say,
"It's a procedure, my dear, to guide your way."

Multiple visits, chemotherapy's embrace,
With each passing day, her hair's fading grace.
But a loving daughter, with words so kind,
Offered a scarf, to her mother's mind.

For months, she bore the weight of her loss,
Without her hair, a heavy cost.
But with time, the healing did start,
Her hair returned, a brand-new part.

Yet, her health grew weaker, a silent toll,
In the face of illness, she'd play her role.
A mother's journey, a family's care,
Through the highs and lows, love was there.

In the past, the battles were won and lost,
But love endured, no matter the cost.
In memories, we find the strength they'd share,
In a mother's love, a family's love, forever to bear.

20. Resolute Love: A Mother's Choice Amidst Illness

In the quiet of the moment, her words did pierce,
A mother's fear, a haunting verse.
"If you take me to the hospital," she'd say,
"I'll surely die," in her own way.

A father's heart, shattered once more,
For the one he loved, his heart he'd pour.
But her stubbornness now took the lead,
She knew what lay ahead, her heart would bleed.

The specter of losing her hair again,
A price too steep, a lingering pain.
She chose to refuse, to stand her ground,
In her silent strength, love was found.

A family's struggle, a cross to bear,
A mother's heart, in love and care.

In the face of illness, a battle they'd fight,
With love as their shield, and hope as their light.

21. A Family United: Navigating Challenges with Love

Four members strong, a family's embrace,
In the midst of challenges, they'd find their grace.
Dad, Mum, elder brother, and their daughter by her side,
Through health's uncertain tide.

A decision made, to stay close at home,
To care of my mum, not to roam.
School would wait, love took its place,
In the circle of family, I'd find my grace.

And silently I carried, a secret to keep,
For my oldest brother, far away, asleep.
Not to burden him, with worries or strife,
In the tapestry of love, I'd navigate life.

Four members united, in love's gentle care,
A family's strength, beyond compare.

Through the highs and lows, together they'd stand,
In the warmth of their love, hand in hand.

22. Persistence in the Face of Illness: A Husband's Love

In pursuit of a cure, a relentless quest,
A husband's love, put to the test.
Consulting doctors, seeking saints' advice,
In the face of illness, a roll of the dice.

Hospitals and temples, paths he'd trod,
In search of answers from a higher God.
Yet, despite his efforts, a resolute stand,
The disease's grip held firm in its hand.

In the face of despair, he'd press on,
A Husband's love, unyielding and strong.
But sometimes, despite all we may do,
Illness has its own course, its own avenue.

Through the journey of hope, he'd strive,
For his beloved wife, to keep her alive.
In the depths of his heart, a love so true,

But the illness persisted, the battle she'd rue.

In the face of uncertainty, love would endure,
A husband's devotion, steadfast and pure.
For sometimes, in life's unpredictable sway,
All we could do was hope and pray.

In the past, his love was unwavering and clear,
A husband's love, through every tear.
Despite the challenges and the pain,
His love for her, forever would remain.

23. Years of Suffering: A Mother's Unyielding Spirit

Years drifted by, pain a constant mate,
In her body's grip, she bore a heavy weight.
Unable to move, each step a painful stride,
Sleep a distant dream, in the night she'd confide.

Lying down brought breathlessness near,
So she'd sit up to sleep, holding back a tear.
A container with a pillow, her makeshift bed,
In the darkness of night, dreams she'd tread.

Sleep eluded her, a restless night's call,
In pain's embrace, she'd find herself thrall.
But through it all, her spirit stayed strong,
In the face of suffering, she'd carry on.

Years as witnesses, her pain we'd see,
A mother's strength, her silent plea.

In her struggle for comfort, for relief,
Her love for her family, beyond belief.

24. Spiritual Guidance and Family Tradition

Grandmother's wisdom, a tale of old,
In mysteries and traditions, her words unfold.
She spoke of black magic, a shadowy art,
A remedy sought, to heal a wounded heart.

"Call a kind soul," she softly said,
"A messenger of peace, with blessings spread.
A warm meal shared, under your roof's embrace,
To dispel the darkness, to find your place."

In Joura, Madhya Pradesh, a temple's call,
To Hanuman, the deity, they'd give their all.
A pilgrimage sought, in faith, they'd go,
To seek protection, and let their worries flow.

Grandmother's guidance, a timeless creed,
In rituals and prayers, they'd find what they need.
For sometimes in faith, they found their way,
Through the night's darkest, to a brighter day.

In the past, her wisdom they'd embrace,
A journey to find solace, in a sacred place.
Through faith and traditions, they'd explore,
And in their hearts, a timeless lore.

25. Mysterious Agarbatti: A Health Crisis Unfolds

In the kitchen's warm embrace, she toiled with care,
A meal prepared, love filled the air.
As she placed the dishes, a kind request made,
A guest in home, in goodwill, he bade.

"Have some food," she gently implored,
In the presence of guest, her spirit soared.
But the visitor's wish, a peculiar plea,
For agarbattis, an offering to be.

With trust and grace, she followed along,
In home, where hearts were strong.
As the incense burned, a ritual begun,
In the air, fragrant prayers did run.

Yet, a sudden shift, a shadow cast,
Over her, a health crisis passed.
Numbness and silence, a throat held tight,
In the midst of guests, a moment of fright.

She longed to speak, to convey her plight,
A trapped voice, a daunting fight.
In the presence of kin, she sought to explain,
The sudden loss of speech, the growing pain.

In that fragile moment, when words would not flow,
A mother's distress, a daughter would know.
The mystery of the agarbatti's role,
In a tale of health, taking its toll.

26. Seeking Solace in Joura: A Family's Journey

In a time of trial, a family's quest,
To Joura they journeyed, in hope's bequest.
Leaving their home, their town behind,
In search of solace, a temple they'd find.

With mother and daughter, they made their way,
In a new place, they'd stay and pray.
The older brother, home did retain,
While dad traveled back and forth, a journey's refrain.

Joura's temple, Hanuman's grace,
A sacred destination, a hallowed place.
In devotion, they sought a way,
To heal, to find strength, in the light of day.

Through the twists and turns of life's design,
In Joura, they'd find solace divine.
In the past, a family's journey they'd share,
A moment in time, marked by love and care.

27. Silent Farewell: A Mother's Passing

On the 5th of May in 2011, a fateful day,
Mother and daughter in a new place they'd stay.
Without husband and son, in that unknown land,
A request from mother, a wish so grand.

"Chant the Bhaktamar Strotra," she'd say,
Her daughter's voice, through the night would sway.
Till midnight, the verses would flow,
In devotion and prayer, their hearts aglow.

Then at 2:37 AM, a moment so still,
Mother held her daughter, a quiet, gentle will.
"I am going tomorrow," she softly declared,
A cryptic message, a secret shared.

With curiosity, her daughter inquired,
"Where are you going?" she desired.
But her mother stayed silent, a knowing nod,
A truth unspoken, a path to God.

Morning arrived, with new medicines near,
A husband's plea, a daughter's fear.
Solid food and water, her daughter tried,
A battle with appetite, on that side.

A shower to cleanse, a routine day,
But a friend's urgent call, a price to pay.
Mother on the floor, a shock to behold,
A life's story, in that moment, was told.

The doctor's arrival, the news so stark,
A mother's passing, a journey in the dark.
In silence, she left, without a goodbye,
A mother's love, forever in the sky.

28. A Son's Urgent Call: Uncovering Family Secrets

On one side, a life had come to its end,
A mother's passing, a message to send.
On the other, a phone call would appear,
A son's wish to speak, a connection so dear.

Father received the call, his eldest son's voice,
A desire to talk, to make a choice.
But mother's promise, to keep her condition concealed,
A silent promise, her love would be revealed.

"Come here," he said, his response calm,
A father's love, like a soothing balm.
He handed the phone to his daughter with grace,
To gently navigate this sensitive space.

Sister spoke, "Mum's resting right now,
Can you wait, my dear? Allow."
Her brother insisted, "I need to speak now,
Ask her to wake up, let's converse somehow."

With patience and love, she'd convince,
To let her rest, her brother's impatience.
A promise to call as she'd awake,
In this delicate moment, love would partake.

Minutes passed, a call once more,
Uncle from nearby, knocking at the door.
"We're heading to your hometown," he inquired,
A chance to return, a situation transpired.

Without a second thought, he agreed to the quest,
A feeling that something wasn't at rest.
In the midst of uncertainty, he'd find his way,
To uncover the truth, come what may.

29. Returning Home: A Son's Regret and Resilience

The eldest son returned, a day after the fall,
To his hometown's embrace, to answer the call.
He couldn't witness, the final goodbye's scene,
The last rites performed, in a moment so keen.

A heavy heart, with regrets in his chest,
The moment he missed, a mother's final rest.
But in the town, he'd find his place,
Amid memories and love, a familiar space.

Though he missed the farewell, the tears that were shed,
In the warmth of his town, his family's spread.
To honor her memory, he'd strive and he'd yearn,
In the lessons she taught, her love he'd discern.

A family once happy, now fractured and torn,
In the face of grief, their hearts would mourn.
The loss of a mother, a presence so dear,

Leaving behind memories, love crystal clear.

In solitude, he found his retreat,
To grapple with grief, in silent defeat.
A slap to the sister, a door tightly closed,
A mother's farewell, a story composed.

He kept it all in, the pain and the ache,
The tears that threatened, the words he'd forsake.
In the stillness of night, he'd find his release,
By closing the door, seeking moments of peace.

A photograph held, in trembling hand,
A connection to her, in that quiet land.
In her smiling face, he'd find his solace,
A memory of love, in a tender embrace.

Words unspoken, emotions concealed,
In the silence, his heart would be revealed.
A mother's love, forever held near,
In the stillness of night, with every tear.

The eldest son, in his quiet retreat,
Took solace in memories, bittersweet.
In the photograph's gaze, her love he'd find,
A bond unbroken, in his heart and mind.

30. Twists of Fate: Love's Anniversary and Farewell

In the tapestry of fate, a tale unfolds,
Of love and loss, where destiny molds,
A story of two hearts, forever entwined,
In the ebb and flow of the hands of time.

Their love, a flame that brightly burned,
On the day of vows, their hearts had yearned,
To share their lives, to walk the same path,
Unaware of the fate's fateful aftermath.

For their anniversary and that day so dear,
Were intertwined, it was perfectly clear,
The day of joy, when their love was blessed,
And the day of sorrow, when she found her rest.

A coincidence that left my father stunned,
As memories of joy and pain became one,
The date of love, their wedding's embrace,
Became the day she left, in heaven's grace.

He, shattered by the twist of destiny's hand,
In grief and love, he had to withstand,
The day he'd said "I do" and "Goodbye,"
A lifetime's worth of emotions to untie.

Yet, in that pain, a lesson we find,
That love endures, in heart and mind,
Their love transcends the bounds of time,
In memories cherished, their spirits climb.

For even in this twist of fate's cruel art,
Their love lives on, in every heart,
A bond unbroken, a love so strong,
In the echoes of their love song.

31. Unseen Efforts, Unheard Love: A Father's Struggle

In shadows cast, a tale untold,
Of blame unjust, a heart of gold,
A father's love, his efforts unseen,
To keep her well, his soul serene.

As whispers swirled, accusing eyes,
No one could fathom the silent cries,
For in his heart, a battle waged,
To save the one he deeply engaged.

He braved the storm of pain and fear,
Each passing day, each falling tear,
He searched for answers, sought the cure,
His love for her, forever pure.

Late nights in solitude, he'd strive,
To find a way, to keep her alive,
Consulting experts, endless quest,

To give her life, his very best.

But little did they know, or see,
The sacrifices, his silent plea,
To keep her well, to ease her pain,
His love for her, an unbroken chain.

The weight of blame, unjust, unkind,
Upon his shoulders, he'd bear in mind,
Yet, in his heart, he'd find the grace,
To protect her memory, in that sacred space.

For in his efforts, love's deep well,
He'd done his utmost, none could tell,
The hero in him, a silent plea,
To keep her safe, forever free.

In the end, when all is said and done,
His love for her forever spun,
A tale of strength, of love so true,
A father's heart, forever new.

32. An Appeal for Understanding and Unity

To those who pointed fingers, placed blame,
Unaware of the grief, the silent shame,
I pen these words, a heartfelt plea,
To see the truth, the pain you couldn't see.

In times of need, when shadows fell,
Your absence spoke, a tale to tell,
Accusations hurled, unfounded, unfair,
When love and support were needed to bear.

You see, my father, in silence, stood,
Defending her with all that he could,
A fortress of love, though unseen,
His battles fought to keep her serene.

Now she's gone, a memory so dear,
Yet the accusations, they still adhere,
But can't you see, it's time to mend,
The wounds you've caused, help hearts to mend?

For blame won't bring her back to life,
Or ease the sorrow, the endless strife,
Instead, let's choose to understand,
The love that he held, hand in hand.

In our pain, we must unite,
Find empathy, bring wrongs to light,
For judgment won't mend wounds so deep,
It's understanding, in which hearts can leap.

So let's stop the blame, the unjust refrain,
And honor her memory without the stain,
Support my father, in his silent plea,
For love and unity is what she'd want to see.

In her absence, let's together stand,
With open hearts, a helping hand,
To heal the wounds that time won't seal,
And find the love in forgiveness, so real.

"Celebrating a life well-lived, 'Enduring Love: A Spouse's Voyage Through Grief' reminds us that in the tapestry of love and loss, the enduring power of family bonds, and the strength to overcome, are what truly make our stories timeless."

www.ingramcontent.com/pod-product-compliance
Lightning Source LLC
La Vergne TN
LVHW041236150826
845673LV00008B/2400

* 9 7 9 8 8 9 1 8 6 4 7 9 5 *